Achieving Your Potential in Christ: Theosis

Plain Talks on a Major Doctrine of Orthodoxy

By Anthony M. Coniaris

Light and Life Publishing Company
P.O. Box 26421
Minneapolis, MN 55426-0421

ISBN 0-937032-93-X

Table of Contents

IV

Achieve Your Potential: Theosis (Part 1)

In the courtyard of our church stands a pool with the words of the Greek palindrome engraved on it: Nipsonanomimatamimono-nopsin, i.e., wash your iniquities not just your face. In the center of the pool stands a bronze sculpture representing a human figure alighting upon the water. As it touches the water with its hand to wash not only its face but also its soul through the tears of repentance, the figure suddenly acquires wings and is about to fly into the heavens.

This sculpture represents our potential as Christians. Through repentance the soul within us sprouts wings and soars to achieve its great potential in Christ, i.e., theosis or union with God.

Let's talk about our great potential as Orthodox Christians. What is it? How can we achieve it?

The Purpose of
Being is to Become

When asked what he thought the business of the Church was, one person said, "It is to show people what they can become by the grace of God." The one thing that holds us back from becoming what God created us to be is sin. That is why the church calls on us constantly to repent: because it is sin that holds us back from greatness, from achieving our great potential of theosis.

My Best Painting
is Yet to be Done

A young artist won an award for a painting of unusual merit. On receiving the award he said to a friend, "That really isn't my best painting." "Oh," said the friend, "then why didn't you exhibit your best?" With a smile he replied, "Because my best painting is yet to be done."

As Christians we are painting pictures of

Jesus with our lives each day. But because we are constantly growing and becoming, the best painting is yet to be. As St. Paul said, "Not as though I had already attained, either were already perfect, but. . . I press on toward the mark" (Phl. 3:12,14).

Simon Peter

When Jesus first met Simon Peter He saw beyond the exterior to the depth of his soul. He knew the kind of person Simon Peter had always been—impetuous, easily influenced, even cowardly. But Jesus saw what He could do in the life of this man, how He could change him from the kind of person he had been and use him for His glory.

So, after gazing at Simon intently, Jesus spoke these words, "You are. . . but you shall become." "You are" expressed the real and actual—what was; "You shall be" referred to the potential—what can be.

That's the way God looks at you and me. He looks at a shepherd boy—David—and sees in him a king. God sees our shortcomings and weaknesses. But He sees beyond these. He sees what we can become through His Son Jesus Christ. He sees our potential to become all that He originally created us to be.

"Jesus looked at him, and said, 'So you are Simon the son of John? You shall be called Cephas'" (which means Peter) John 1:42. You are! You shall be! The actual and the possible! Realism and idealism! What is and what can be. And between the two, the Lord Jesus Christ. His presence is like a mighty bridge spanning the vast chasm between the actual and the potential.

We are Human Becomings

Like Michelangelo who looked at a rough, shapeless stone and saw a statue of David in it, Jesus was constantly looking at people in terms of what they can become. We may be defeated, degraded, soiled, enslaved by our passions, yet through Christ we can be saved, cleansed of all unrighteousness, and clothed in the beauty of holiness and service. Jesus can take our potential and convert it into reality. The purpose of being is not to remain as we are but to become.

"We are not yet human beings; we are human becomings," someone said. "To become what we are capable of becoming is the only end of life," said Robert Louis Stevenson. Louis Pasteur said, "When I approach a child, he inspires in me two sentiments: tenderness for what he is, and respect for what he may become." Someone asked a boy, "Who made you, Sonny?" And the boy replied, "To tell you the truth, sir, I ain't done yet."

Power to Become

God gives us power to become: "To all who received him. . . He gave power to become children of God" (Jn. 1:12). The Apostle Peter once came upon a lame man begging for alms. He walked up to the cripple and said, "Silver and gold I have done but in the name of the Lord I say to thee, Rise and walk!" That is the kind of power Christ gives us—power to get up and walk out of a crippled past into a life of power, meaning, peace and joy; power to become better than we are; power to become new creatures in Christ Jesus; power to become gods by grace, partakers of divine nature, heirs of His kingdom.

Psychiatry can tell us what is wrong with us but only Christ can give us the power to rise out of sin and sickness to become what we ought to be and can be: children of God and gods by grace.

Power to Ascend Spiritually

Before Darwin, people believed that creation had ceased. God had created the world long ago and had stopped. After Darwin, people came to realize that God has not finished the creation of the world. He is still creating. This is part of what theistic evolution is. Our own creation is still going on. Man is evolving intellectually. Everything from the Ford automobile to the Einstein equation has been created in the past 100 years. Tielhard De Chardin, the great anthropologist, believed that the destiny of man is to rise toward spiritual perfection until at last he is united with God. God has given us the power to become better than we are. He has given us the ability and the grace to evolve not only intellectually but also spiritually. We do not have to be captured by our past or by our smallness or by our sins. With God's power we can rise to new heights of intellectual and spiritual perfection. The ladder of divine ascent is there for us to ascend, to climb each day, that we may achieve theosis and be united with God.

Bishop Maximos Aghiorgoussis writes, "The fathers make a distinction between the image of God in man, and his likeness to God; image is the potential given to man, through which he can obtain the life of theosis (communion with God). Likeness with God is the actualization of this potential; it is becoming more and more what one already is: becoming more and more God's image, more and more God-like. The distinction between image and likeness is, in other words, the distinction between being and becoming."*

Achieve Your Potential

A modern psychologist writes:

"It is part of the tragedy of the human situation that the development of the self is never completed; even under the best conditions only part of man's potential is realized. Man always dies before he is fully born.

"Man's main task in life is to give birth to himself, to become what he potentially is."

Achieving the Ideal

Many of us go through life wishing for the ideal—the ideal parent, the ideal child, the

---

* "Salvation in Christ - A Lutheran-Orthodox Dialogue," John Meyendorff and Robert Tobias. Augsburg Publ. House, Minneapolis, MN. 1992.

ideal husband or wife. We forget that none of us is a finished product, complete like a piece of beautiful china. Each of us is in the process of becoming. How many divorces occur because there is a foolish idea in our minds that some perfect mate exists somewhere: and that we must shed the present mate to find the perfect one. We forget that the perennial problem in marriage is not to find the ideal partner, but to become the ideal partner. It is this power to become better than we are, a new creation, sons and daughters of God, gods by grace, that Christ offers to those who receive Him and believe in Him; power to overcome the world; power to crucify every besetting sin; power to shout in triumph over every trouble and temptation in life, "I can do all things through Christ who strengthens me"; power to become what we are by baptism: children of God, heirs of God's kingdom.

Salvation: A Matter of Becoming

Salvation according to Orthodox theology is not a state of being but a state of becoming, a constant movement toward union with God (theosis) which can never be fully achieved in this life. It is a process that begins here and is consummated and perfected in heaven.

Never would the saints of the church say, "I am saved. I have made it. I have arrived." They were always on the way. So they kept praying the Jesus Prayer to the very end: "Lord Jesus, Son of God, have mercy on me, the sinner." The Christian life is constant growth, constant becoming, a constant journey from being the image of God, to becoming the likeness of God.

Speaking of this ongoing growth toward theosis, Vladimir Lossky writes,

The deification or theosis of the creature will be realized in its fullness only in the age to come, after the resurrection of the dead. This deifying union has, nevertheless, to be fulfilled ever more

and more even in this present life, through the transformation of our corruptible and depraved nature and by its adaptation to eternal life.[*]

A Constant Conversion

The great saints of the church were humble men and women who radiated God's grace and love. They were not converted just once. They were not "born again" just once. Nor did they repent just once. Their life was a daily conversion and a constant repentance. They were saved once at the cross of Golgotha, but they were also being saved daily in the yielding of their will to Jesus. Daily they sinned and daily they repented. Daily they fell and daily they rose.

The Beginning Not the End

Fundamentalist Christians are constantly

---

[*] "The Mystical Theology of the Eastern Church." V. Lossky. James Clarke and Co. Cambridge and London, 1968. P. 196.

proclaiming on radio and TV that all we have to do to be saved is make a "decision" for Christ and be "born again" by believing in Jesus. They tell us that one becomes a full and complete Christian as soon as this happens. The whole process of growth is thereby omitted. One goes immediately from the cradle to mature spiritual adulthood. Orthodoxy believes that to confess faith in Christ is the beginning not the end. It is a journey, not a bed on which to lie while we wait for the Lord's return. The moment we become like the Pharisee and say, "I have arrived. I am where I am supposed to be. I thank God I am not like the others"—at that point we become stagnant and stagnation in the spiritual life is condemnation.

Only God has Arrived

Human perfection is not the state of "having arrived." Only God has arrived. Only God is perfect in this sense. Human perfection consists in a constant growing toward perfection, a constant journey from the image of God to the likeness of God, a constant "becoming" as St. Gregory of Nyssa says when he speaks of "the eternal discovery of the eternal growing."

St. Gregory Palamas believed that even in the age to come, the saints' vision of God will not be static. He writes,

"Clearly it will develop infinitely... The saints, communing in the grace of God and rendered through that communion more and more able to contain the divine radiance, will receive grace upon grace from God Himself, its infinite and unfailing source."

Orthodox Christians, for example, are named after saints because once we are baptized achieving sainthood (which is a fruit of theosis) becomes our potential and our goal.

Fr. Thomas Hopko writes,

St. Gregory said that there are two differences between God and us: "God is the archetype and we are the image";

"God is the Being, and the Super Being, and we are becoming," that is, "God is an inexhaustible abyss and we are an inexhaustible possibility of growth." Therefore the human spirit is as inexhaustible as the Being of God because it is created in the image of God. The growth in perfection is, thus, the human perfection. It is not as if, "keep on trying and some day you will be perfect," but Gregory of Nyssa said, when you try, when you are growing, then you are perfect. Then you are as perfect as a human can be, because the growth is perfection, the movement toward perfection, is in fact what it means for the human to be perfect...Whatever stage you reach there is literally an infinity of possibility for growth still before you. And according to the Fathers, this goes on for all eternity, even in the Kingdom of God. That is the character of what it means to be created in the image and likeness of God.

Achieve Your Potential: Theosis (Part 2)

We are saved from sin for theosis.

On a nationally syndicated call-in television program, two interview guests—both doctors—were discussing the subject of abortion. Addressing the doctor who was against abortion, a young female caller expressed the opinion that the human fetus was not really a human being at all, only potential human life.

The doctor echoed the words of the Psalmist as he responded almost thunderously, "Ma'am, that's not potential human life. That's human life with great potential."

There is Greatness in Us

The Bible tells us that it was God who formed us in our mother's womb. And when He formed us He placed within us the highest possible potential: theosis, union with God. Part of man's tragedy is that this great potential remains only a potential and is not fully developed. Man is indeed a frail creature but he is endowed by God with a fantastically great potential. Ralph Waldo Emerson said, "What lies behind us, and what lies before us, are small matters compared to what lies within us." All of us are born equal. Our job is to outgrow equality by reaching out to achieve our potential in Christ. There is greatness in us!

Your Best Friend

Henry Ford was having lunch with a friend one day. The friend asked him, "Who is your best friend?" Ford took out a pen and wrote on the white napkin before him these words, "Your best friend is the person who brings out of you the best that is within you." That makes Christ your best Friend. That makes the Church your best friend. That makes the Bible your best friend. For their purpose is to help you achieve the great potential God has placed within you.

Gloria Steinem, feminist leader, said once, "By the year 2000 we will, I hope, raise our children to believe in human potential, not God." Human potential not God! The truth is that without God you not only lose your human potential; you end up in hell. With God, your potential becomes heaven itself where "eye has not seen what things God has prepared for those who love Him."

The tragedy for most of us is that we die before we are fully born. We die with so much unlived life in us. We have a hundred acres of possibilities and only about one-half acre under cultivation. We are a picture of unfulfillment. As Oliver Wendell Holmes said, "Many people die with their music still in them."

"Amartia": Missing the Mark

In the New Testament the word for sin is Amartia. Translated literally from Greek it does not mean "to break a rule." It means rather "to miss the mark," "to miss the target, the bull's eye." That is the great tragedy of sin which occurs when a person doesn't measure up to his or her full potential and fails to become all that God created him to be. Thus sin is to miss the target, to fail to claim and develop the fantastic potential God has placed in us. For, man is not only hell bent, the potential God has placed in us makes us also—and even more so—heaven bent. As St. Paul writes in Rom. 5:20, "Where sin abounded, grace abounded all the more."

Theosis: Our Potential

Orthodox theology calls the potential for which God created us: THEOSIS. Don't be frightened by this word. It's really a very simple concept, namely, the core of the good news of Orthodoxy is what we are called to share in the very life of God. Salvation in Orthodox theology is much more positive than it is negative. It means not only justification and forgiveness of sins; it means also—and even more so—the renewing and restoration of God's image in us, the lifting up of fallen humanity through Christ into the very life of God. Christ forgives us and frees us from sin and death that we may proceed to fulfill our potential, which is to become like God in Christ and to share in His life.

Christ came to save us from sin for participation in the life of God. In other words, we are saved from sin for theosis, which is our great potential.

Jesus came to earth to tell us:

"You give me your time, and I will give you my eternity. You give me your weary body, and I will give you rest. You give me your sins, and I will give you forgiveness. You give me your broken heart, and I will give you healing. You give me your emptiness, and I will give you my fulness. You give me your humanity, and I will give you my divinity."

Theosis:
Positive Aspect of Salvation

Theosis is the positive aspect of salvation. To describe theosis we can use the following words:

- transfiguration of man,
- putting on Christ,
- the restoration of the image of God in us,
- restoration of communion with God,
- participation in the life of God,
- incorruption,
- receiving the Holy Spirit,
- becoming temples of the Holy Spirit,
- ascending to the throne of God,
- participating in the kingdom of God,
- being by grace what God is by nature.

Theosis is. . .

To describe further what our potential—theosis—is, we can say the following:

Jesus came to lift the fallen all the way from the gutter of sin to the throne of God in theosis.

Theosis is what God wants for us who are created in His own image: to become like Him in whose image we are made.

Theosis is a personal sharing in the life of God through faith, prayer and the sacraments.

Theosis is the rich potential God has placed in each baptized person.

Theosis is the name for the process of salvation, initiated in baptism, by which we are Christified, i.e., united to Christ and changed into His likeness.

Theosis is the transfiguration of our lifestyle, implying concern for our neighbor, mutual sharing, love, stewardship of ourselves, of our possessions and of the earth.

Fr. George Florovsky wrote, "Theosis means no more than an intimate communion of human persons with the living God. To be with God means to dwell in Him and to share His perfection."

Saved for Theosis

Christ the Savior came to redeem us from sin that we might proceed to acquire the gift of theosis which He offers us by grace. Salvation does not end with the forgiveness of sins; it begins there. It is at baptism that our journey to God, to theosis, begins. Salvation is not only a matter of "Are you saved?" It is also a matter of "Are you being deified? Are you growing in Christ?" We are saved from sin for theosis. "Original sin," said Fr. George Florovsky, "was not just an erroneous choice. . . but rather a refusal to ascend toward God."

We are saved from sin for theosis. Salvation is an ongoing process that leads from initial salvation in baptism, through sanctification, and on to "deification by grace."

From Egypt to the Promised Land

Vladimir Lossky said, "What does it matter being saved from death, from Hell, if it is not to lose oneself in God." St. John Chrysostom said, "It is not enough to leave Egypt (sin and death), one must also enter the Promised Land (theosis). Between Egypt and the Promised Land lies a desert." Hence the need for ascesis (struggle, discipline, war against the passions) in our journey through the desolate desert of sin and death toward theosis (the promised land).

Theosis is a beautiful word but what does it say to those who are trying to cope with a terrible illness, or struggling to make a go of a sour marriage, or to those who are burdened with anxieties and cares? Theosis has everything to say to struggling humanity. It tells us that we have the capacity through the presence of God within us to transcend and overcome any and every difficulty in life, including the greatest one of all: death. Theosis tells us that we are not paupers or beggars but sons and daughters of God, sharing His glory, partaking of His Nature, destined to inherit His eternal kingdom. Theosis tells us that we are more than conquerors through Him Who loved us. Theosis tells us to "hang in there" no matter how hard the struggle or the temptation because God has great things in store for us. As St. Paul says, " I consider that the sufferings of this present time are not worth comparing with the glory that is to be revealed to us" (Romans 8:18).

Prayer

Lord, thank You for the tremendous potential You gave us by grace when we were baptized. Sustain us, strengthen us, uphold us in our journey from the slavery of Egypt to the promised land of theosis. Amen.

Achieving Our Potential in Christ: Theosis (Part 3)

At baptism we sing the beautiful words of St. Paul, "As many as were baptized in Christ have put on Christ. Alleluia."

The fact that at baptism we have "put on Christ" has tremendous implications. If we have put on Christ, then we have put on His love, His forgiveness, His peace, His joy. If we have put on Christ, we have put on His servanthood: "If I your Lord and Master have washed your feet, then you also ought to wash one another's feet." If we have put on Christ, then we shall suffer as Christ suffered; we shall be persecuted for the truth as Christ was persecuted. If we have put on Christ, we shall be resurrected as Jesus was. We shall be glorified as Christ was glorified; we shall ascend to the Father as He ascended to the Father. We shall sit at the right hand of the Father with Jesus. We shall partake of His divine nature and share in His life and glory, becoming "gods by grace" as He is God by nature and essence.

Thus, theosis began for us in baptism. When we were baptized we "put on Christ," i.e., we received the life of Christ within us, the same life that enabled Christ to walk this earth for 33 years without sinning. Thus, on the day of our baptism, we became new persons, with a brand new potential: theosis or union with God.

It Has Already Happened

Theosis is not something new. It has already occurred at the Transfiguration when the human body of Jesus was transfigured and shone more brightly than the sun. Here we see the great potential of human nature in Christ. Here we see the potential spirituality of man in its highest form! Here we see the dust of the flesh transfigured into God's likeness in divine glory! Here we see the human body as God originally created it to be—radiant, resplendent and glorious! Here we see what human nature can again become in Christ by God's grace.

The following troparia of the Feast of the Transfiguration bring this out:

"Transfigured today on Mount Tabor in His disciples' presence, Christ revealed the original beauty of the image...

"Transfigured, You have made Adam's nature, which had grown dim, to shine once more as lightning, transforming it into the glory and splendor of your Godhead."

"I'm Only Human!"

How often we hear people trying to excuse their sins and failures by saying, "I'm only human!" You are human, but God became human in Christ to show us what it really means to be human. To be human means to be able to share in God's life. To be human means to have the Holy Spirit dwelling in our bodies, making them temples of God. To be human means to have the Lord Jesus sitting on the throne of our heart, making us palaces of God's presence. To be truly human means to be able in Christ to transcend human weaknesses and frailties and to become like Christ in whose image we were created.

One who is truly human:
truly fulfills God's commandments—
he makes his body a throne for his mind,
his mind a throne for spirit,
and his spirit a throne for soul.
Then his soul too becomes a throne
for the light of the Presence
that rests upon him.
The light spreads forth around him,
and he, at the center of that light,
trembles in his joy.

— Hasidic Saying

Spiritual Dwarfs

But all of this presupposes ascesis, struggle and constant growth in the life of Christ.

Without this ascesis and constant spiritual growth, not only do we not attain our potential—theosis—but we also become moral and spiritual pygmies or dwarfs. Leslie Brandt writes:

There is a method of stunting trees so that
they never grow higher than a couple
of feet.
It is done by tying off the taproot so that
the tree is forced to live off its surface
roots.
These trees beautify unique little gardens
making them places of supreme beauty,
but perform little service beyond that.
They are rather useless in terms of
supplying lumber for building or for
shelter against raging typhoons.
They become potted plants instead of the
forest giants they were originally
intended to be.

A baby in a crib is a beautiful sight to
behold, but if that creature, plagued by
some crippling disease, remains a crib-
baby after twelve or fifteen years, it
becomes a tragic and pitiful sight indeed.

Even more tragic, though of far less concern to people, are the moral and spiritual dwarfs who have never attained to the height and stature they are destined for and who are potted plants instead of forest giants because their taproots are tied off and they have never gone deep into an intimate relationship with God to draw on divine sustenance and strength. *

Created to be giants we end up as dwarfs when the taproot, designed for an in-depth relationship with God, is cut off and we live on the surface of life.

Fr. Alexander Elchaninov writes,

"The man who denies his relationship with God, who refuses to be His Son, is not a real man but a man stunted, the unfinished plan of a man. For to be sons of God is not only granted us as a gift but is also entrusted to us as a task, and only the accomplishment of this task, through the conscious putting on

* "Christ in Your Life," L. Brandt. Concordia Publ. Co., St. Louis Mo. 1980. P. 140.

of Christ and God, can lead to a full disclo-
sure, a full blossoming, of each human per-
sonality.*

Our Main Aim in Life

It is no wonder that the Orthodox Church
considers our aim in life to be union with
God and theosis! We were created to share in
God's life. This is what makes us different
from animals. We were created to be recepta-
cles of God's life, without which we cease to
be truly human.

When someone asked an Orthodox priest
one day what he thought was the main em-
phasis of the Orthodox Church, he replied
with one word, "Theosis." And he was right.

It is said that the greatest compliment God
ever paid man was when He said to him, "Be
ye perfect as your heavenly Father is perfect."

---

* "The Diary of a Russian Priest," A. Elchaninov. P. 44. Faber and
Faber. London. 1967.

Let Loose the Slumbering Christ Within You

Leslie Newbigin said once, "I know and believe that each person I see, has a capacity to let loose in him the Risen Christ, now often slumbering but there incontrovertibly..." To let loose the Christ who is within you, will be the beginning of a personal transformation and transfiguration that will be nothing less than theosis, union with God.

Two Caterpillars

Two caterpillars sat watching a butterfly flying overhead. After some time, one caterpillar remarked to the other, "You wouldn't get me up in one of those things for a million dollars!"

Of course, the unsuspecting caterpillar was little aware that he was gazing upon his own future destiny. My hope through these talks on theosis is that you will catch a glimpse of your own future destiny. For we are destined to share in Christ's glory. His victory over death was our victory over death. His Pascha, His resurrection, has become our Pascha, our resurrection. His transfiguration, our transfiguration. His ascension, our ascension. His glorification, our glorification.

The Seedling's Strength

I read recently that the strength exerted by a tiny little plant as it pushes its stem above the ground's surface is roughly 450 pounds per square inch. Four hundred and fifty pounds of pressure in those delicate little plants pushing their way above ground!

I was amazed and awed by the power God has placed even in the tiniest of His creations. And then I thought to myself: If God has given an organism the size of my fingernail such strength, how much more energy must I have within myself, untapped?

Indeed, God has placed untapped reservoirs of strength within us to enable us to attain theosis and union with Him. Think of prayer, the Bible and all the sacraments, especially the Eucharist. These are all ways for us to achieve theosis, union with God.

In many ways we are like a chick within an eggshell. Awakening to the fact that he is cramped in the shell and needs food and space, he begins to peck his way out. Suddenly he discovers a brand new world of freedom, light and food.

You Have a
Rendezvous with Glory

We live much of our lives as if in a shell. We are forever like the chick and his shell—within an inch of true life and living.

Within each one of us God has placed the capacity for unlimited growth. Yours is the privilege of giving birth to this new potential, this new life by breaking out of your shell. You have a rendezvous with glory. You have a rendezvous with fullness of life in Christ! You have a rendezvous with "Christ in you, the hope of glory" (Gal. 1:27). You have a rendezvous with greatness!

Vladimir Soloviev, a Russian religious philosopher, wrote,

"Your tendencies and ambitions come from God. They are remote calls from His kindness. . . If you wish to be upraised unto God, if you wish to be so united with God, that God is all in you, if you despair because, eager to share in the divine nature, you have a glimpse of it in its inaccessible infinity, then, take assurance. The Father, the Son and the Holy Spirit are calling you, indeed, to ascend unto Them.

"They are ready to come down towards you and in you, in order to live as the habitual guests of your soul. They promise to your whole being, in exchange for what is good in it, a transformation, at first mysterious and invisible, but soon resplendent and glorious, a union and assimilation that will divinize

you."

It is important that we keep the spark alive in us.

A person at prayer is like a bed of coals,
As long as a single spark remains,
a great fire can be kindled.
But without that spark there can be no fire.

Always remain attached to God,
even in those times
when you feel unable to ascend to Him.
You must preserve that single spark—
lest the fire of your soul be extinguished
— Hasidic saying.

Achieving Your Potential in Christ: Theosis (Part 4)

Achieving your potential in Christ means that you become what you are. St. Gregory of Sinai expressed this well when he wrote,

> *Become what you already are,*
> *Find Him who is already yours,*
> *Listen to Him who never ceases*
> *speaking to you,*
> *Own Him who already owns you.*

Every living thing on earth shares a common need—to fulfill its purpose, its potential. The acorn's potential, for example, is to become an oak tree. The puppy, to become a dog. The kitten, a cat. The caterpillar, a butterfly. Each of these has a need to become what it is meant to be.

Does the acorn have to beg God to become an oak tree? No! Does the puppy have to whine and plead to God to make him a dog? Certainly not! God wants them to grow and reach their full potential.

God Wants Us to Achieve Our Potential

And the same thing is true of us. In baptism God planted within us a great potential, i.e., union with God, theosis. Not only does God want us to achieve that potential but He will also help us achieve that potential if we cooperate with Him, traveling the road of Christian ascesis and discipline as we walk with Christ and follow Him.

Our goal is a deeper sharing in the life of God, to become like Him whom we love and worship. And having been given the Holy Spirit, that goal becomes possible for us. We need, then, to set our sights high. We need to shoot for the stars, to aim for theosis, that we may achieve our potential which is to realize the fullness of the image of God in us. John Breck writes, "The ultimate goal and meaning of human existence is not only 'to love God and enjoy Him forever' but also to share fully in the glory of His divine life."

Meister Eckhart expressed this well when

he wrote:

> *"The seed of God is in us.*
> *Given an intelligent and*
> *hard-working farmer,*
> *it will thrive and grow up to God,*
> *whose seed it is;*
> *and accordingly its fruits will be*
> *God-nature.*
> *Pear seeds grow into pear trees,*
> *nut seeds into nut trees and*
> *God seed into God."*

It is our task then to become what we are as the image and likeness of God: to share more fully in the life of God.

Jonathan Livingston Seagull

Some years ago there was a book entitled, "Jonathan Livingston Seagull." Jonathan Livingston Seagull was no ordinary bird! He began life as one of the Breakfast Flock, whose members flew merely to eat. But suspecting that a seagull was created to seek more than a breakfast, Jonathan persisted in flying for the beauty of flying, for the perfection of it, and for the experience of pure freedom. His parents were worried when they saw the direction their son was going, and they warned him, "If you must study, then study food, and how to get it. This fancy flying business is all very well, but you can't eat a glide, you know. Don't forget that the reason you fly is to eat."

But something inside Jonathan drove him back to his study of flying. He finally achieved a breakthrough, learning about the loop, the slow roll, the point roll, the inverted spin, the full bunt, the pinwheel. He imagined how delighted the rest of the flock would be when they learned of his discoveries. "Instead of slogging back and forth to the fishing boats," he told himself, "there's a reason to life! We can lift ourselves out of ignorance, we can find ourselves as creatures of excellence and intelligence and skill. We can be free! We can learn to fly!"

Hearing this, Maynard Gull said to Jonathan, "Are you saying that I can fly?" and Jonathan said, "I say you are free." Then

Maynard Gull spread his wings and lifted into the dark night, and the whole flock aroused from sleep by his cry as loud as he could scream from five hundred feet up, "I can fly! Listen, I can fly." And Jonathan turned to the rest of the flock and said, "You can fly, too." And they answered "How do you expect us to fly as you fly? You are a special and gifted bird." And they mentioned a few other gifted birds, and Jonathan said, "The only difference is that they have begun to understand what they really are and begun to practice it."

When we were baptized, God gave each one of us spiritual wings. They are prayer, faith, hope, the Bible, the Sacraments, the Holy Spirit, and his inner presence. We are to use them to fly above the clouds of hopelessness and defeat. We are to use them to soar to the heights of what God created us to be.

The reason for living is not just working in order to eat. It is far higher: "Now we are the children of God, but it does not yet appear what we shall be. For when He (Christ) appears we shall be like Him. We shall see Him as He is" (Apostle John). There is no more miserable person than the one who goes through life and realizes he has not achieved his full potential. He has denied what he could be.

Living Examples of Theosis: The Saints

Theosis is not just a dogma, a teaching of the Church. It becomes a living reality in the Theotokos and the saints of the church. Theosis takes on flesh and blood and becomes real in the saints who have been justified and sanctified and are thereby sons and daughters of the resurrection. The saints are "gods by participation" reflecting the light and love of Christ in their lives. The lives of the saints and their icons shine with the presence of God and serve to remind us of our high calling: to become gods by grace, "having been delivered from the bondage of corruption and death into the glorious liberty of the children of God" (Rom. 8:21).

The Icons and Theosis

The icons depict not only God becoming man in Christ, but also man becoming god by grace. In other words, the icons give us a foretaste of our own deification, our own theosis, our own sharing in the life of God, our own glorification. That is why the saints are depicted in the icons not only in their human state but more especially in their transfigured, deified state. They have already attained theosis, union with God. They are already sharing in the life of God.

Theosis: Visible Sign of Salvation

Theosis is a visible sign of our salvation in Christ. It demonstrates that we are already partaking of the grace of God in this world. By looking at the saints we are able to see salvation at work and in action. Fr. A. Calivas says, "The saints are the concrete evidence of the transfiguring power of the Gospel. They are the first fruits of the heavenly life, the forerunners of the kingdom of God." The saints are also concrete evidence of the reality of theosis.

When someone asks you, "Are you saved?" The Orthodox answer would be, "Yes. I'm saved and I'm now on the way to theosis, to sainthood, to sharing more fully in the life of God."

Prayer

Remove the garbage of sin from our lives, dear Lord. Eliminate the weight of sin that keeps us earthbound. Like Jonathan Livingston Seagull, help us to soar to the heavenly heights for which You created us. Help us to shoot for the stars, for that is our destiny. Enable us by Your grace to grow and become what we are. As the pear seed grows into a pear tree, so may the God seed You planted in us at baptism grow to become Your divine likeness as in the saints. Amen.

How is Theosis Achieved?
(Part 5)

I found a beautiful Biblical description of the state of Theosis in Psalm 27:

"One thing have I asked of the Lord,
    that will I seek after;
that I may dwell in the house of the Lord
    all the days of my life,
to behold the beauty of the Lord,
    and to inquire in his temple.

For He will hide me in his shelter
    in the day of trouble;
He will conceal me under the cover
    of his tent,
He will set me high upon a rock."
            — Psalm 27: 4-5

We come now to the question: How is theosis possible?

It is the Incarnation, God becoming man in Christ, that opens the way to theosis, union with God. Christ put on our humanity that we might put on His divinity—"Christ in you, the hope of glory," writes Paul. God became man in Christ in order to open up the possibility of theosis, man/woman transcending their humanity and sharing in the life of God. In becoming man, Christ empowered us to share in His own divine nature. The Holy Spirit, sent by the Father into our hearts, fills us ever more and more with divine life and power.

St. Symeon the New Theologian says, "What then is the purpose of the Incarnation... if not to let us share in what was His after His sharing in what is ours?" Elsewhere he writes, "He became poor so that you might become rich, to let you share in the richness of His grace. That is why He assumed flesh, that you might become partakers of His divinity."

Fr. Henri Nouwen writes,

The great mystery is that Jesus, in whom the fullness of God dwells, has become our home. Through Jesus, God has entered the intimacy of our innermost self, so that we can enter into God's own intimacy. This is the mystery of the incarnation: by taking our flesh God made a home in us. Thus we are clothed with divinity and find our home in God.*

Baptism

The chief instruments in achieving theosis are the sacraments. Let's look at them briefly beginning with Baptism.

St. Gregory of Nazianzos writes, "The Holy Spirit divinizes (deifies) the person who is baptized." Baptism, according to Orthodox theology, does more than set us free from the bondage of original sin, it clothes us with Christ and makes us partakers of His divine nature. Hence the singing during the baptismal service of the verse from the letter of Paul to the Galatians, "As many of you as have been baptized in Christ have put on Christ."

At a certain point in the baptismal service,

---

* Sojourners, 16 June 1985. P. 17

the celebrant priest says to the newly baptized, "You are baptized. You are illumined. You are anointed with Holy Chrism. You are sanctified. You are washed in the name of the Father and the Son and the Holy Spirit." We may add to these words the expression of St. Gregory of Sinai: "Become what you already are," i.e., claim the gift of theosis that God has given you in Holy Baptism and develop it as you go through life. Grow in the life of Christ which you have received in Baptism that you may become a true son or daughter of the heavenly Father.

Holy Chrismation

After baptism the next aid to theosis is the Sacrament of Holy Chrismation which is our personal Pentecost. Through this sacrament we are anointed and sealed with the gift of the Holy Spirit. Theosis is a gift from God the Father, through God the Son, in God the Holy Spirit. Through this sacrament (Chrismation) the Holy Spirit comes to activate and vivify the new life which the newly baptized has received in Christ. It is this miracle of the presence of the Holy Spirit within us that allows us to grow continually toward theosis in and through God's love and grace. We are made "partakers of divine nature" through Baptism and the seal of the gift of the Holy Spirit. We must pray daily for the infilling of the Holy Spirit, using that beautiful Orthodox prayer to the Holy Spirit, "Heavenly King, Comforter, Spirit of Truth... come and pitch your tent in me."

The Eucharist

In addition to Baptism and Chrismation, we are made "partakers of divine nature" through the Eucharist which unites us with God. St. Gregory of Nyssa writes, "He (Christ) sows Himself in the bodies of the faithful by means of his own Body which is composed of bread and wine. He thus is comingled with us, so that by our union with the immortal, we might share in immortality."

The Eucharist truly makes us "partakers of divine nature" when we receive "with the fear of God, with faith, and with love" the presence of Christ as it comes to us veiled under the bread and the wine. It is truly a life-giving (zoopoion) sacrament, imparting to us the very life of God through Jesus who is the living Bread (artos zoes). In receiving the deified flesh of our Savior, we too are deified as we receive the gifts and grace of theosis. Fr. Christopher Stavropoulos writes, "Through the Holy Eucharist, we are made divine... the person who communes... is invisibly fed and concurrently receives the seed of immortality and the resurrection from the dead."

By participating in the life of the Church, Orthodox Christians are now being divinized as they receive the Bread of Life, the Medicine of Immortality, the Precious Body and Blood of Christ. It is to receive this wondrous gift of salvation and theosis that we come so regularly to the manger of the Divine Liturgy.

Prayer

In addition to Baptism, Chrismation and the Eucharist, the next way by which we are made "partakers of divine nature" and achieve theosis is through prayer.

Theosis cannot happen without prayer. The Church Fathers say about prayer: "The power of prayer fulfills (completes) the sacrament of our union with God... Prayer uplifts and unites human beings with God" (St. Gregory Palamas). "The effect of prayer is union with God" (St. Gregory Nyssa). "Sacred prayer, and it alone... joins God with man, and makes the two one spirit."

"Touching the Ceiling"

When the actor, Anthony Quinn, was being interviewed on a television program, he was asked "You're in your 70's now. You've starred in so many movies. You've won Oscars. How do you feel about it? What is life all about for you?"

Quinn replied, "I have not touched the ceiling yet." For us Orthodox Christians "touching the ceiling" is to begin to experience now the fruits of theosis, union with God through prayer and the sacraments.

"Touching the ceiling" has been made possible through Christ who became one with us that we might become one with Him. And, indeed, we do become one with Him in theosis through:

1. Baptism by which we are clothed with Christ;
2. Chrismation by which the Holy Spirit comes to dwell in us, vivifying the new life we received in Baptism;
3. The Eucharist through which we receive the Presence of Christ within us;
4. Prayer which completes our union with God and makes us one spirit.

Prayer

Blessed Trinity, Father, Son and Holy

Spirit, thank You for making it possible for us to "touch the ceiling" of life through theosis which You have made possible for us through Your Incarnation, through Baptism, Chrismation, the Eucharist and Prayer. Help us daily to claim and develop this great gift which will one day usher us into Your presence where we shall see You as You are and be like You. Amen.

Our Potential in Christ: Theosis (Part 6)

Thoughts on Theosis from the Hymns of the Feast of the Transfiguration

Today Christ on Mount Tabor has changed the darkened nature of Adam, and filling it with brightness He has made it godlike (Transfiguration Troparion)

Christ came to make our humanity god-like, the way it would have been without the fall of Adam. He gave us a humanity that is surpassed in that which it is called to become when it shares in the glory of God.

He who once spoke through symbols to Moses on Mount Sinai, saying, 'I am He who is,' was transfigured today upon Mount Tabor before the disciples; and in His own person He showed them the nature of man, arrayed in the original beauty of the image (Transfiguration Troparion).

Christ restored the positive beauty of the original image of God that had been marred by sin and prepared it for theosis.

Thou wast transfigured upon Mount Tabor, showing the exchange mortal men will make with Thy glory at Thy second and fearful coming, O Saviour (Transfiguration Troparion).

This means that the bodies of our loved ones now buried will be raised at the second coming as transfigured and glorified bodies. As St. Paul writes, "It (the body) is sown in dishonor, it is raised in glory" (I Cor. 18:43).

Thou hast put Adam on entire, O Christ, and changing the nature grown dark in past times, Thou has filled it with glory and made it godlike (Transfiguration Troparion.)

Our destiny is theosis, deification, union with Christ. As we live in Christ and for Christ, the result is the surpassing of the created in communion with the uncreated.

Repentance

In addition to prayer there can be no theosis without repentance. Theosis keeps producing within us an increased sensitivity to sin which leads to a continual attitude of repentance.

St. John of the Ladder says that repentance is a renewal of our baptism, a new birth, a new resurrection, a new creation. He goes on to say that repentance is "a turning point from that which is not our nature, to that which is our nature, and a turning from the devil to God through spiritual struggle and pain."

St. James the Syrian said, "Repentance is the door of mercy, open to those who seek it diligently. By this door (of repentance) we enter into Divine mercy, and by no other entrance we can find this mercy. Let us not grieve when we make a slip, but to be hardened in the same slip means total death."

Ascesis

All of the above mentioned means toward theosis—prayer, the sacraments, repentance—require our cooperation. This cooperation is expressed in Orthodox theology by the word ascesis, which may be defined as a constant, persistent striving toward the goal of theosis. The aim of ascesis or struggle is never to gain merit, or payment or reward from God. It represents the struggle that is involved in renouncing our sinful will in order to yield ourselves totally to God in self-surrender as we journey toward theosis or union with Him.

Ascesis and Crucifixion

Ascesis must be viewed in the light of the crucifixion. Christ did not die instead of us, so that we would not have to die. He died for us, so that we could die with Him, and in dying with Him, have life. His is the only death that leads to life. Our death, our dying to sin, apart from His, does not lead to life. But in Baptism, Jesus draws us into His own dying (Rom. 6:3). This dying with Christ in order to rise with Him is what we Orthodox mean by ascesis.

Through ascesis we are called to die to sin and self so that we may live the life of God. We must become "dead indeed unto sin, but alive unto God through Jesus Christ our Lord" (Rom 6:11). Such ascesis is not limited to the practice of certain specific rituals such as fasting, vigils, prayer, etc., it is rather a whole way of life. To deny ourselves in this way is part of the ascesis, the training for theosis. Such ascesis serves to conform us to the image of God as we grow toward theosis.

Love as the Means of Theosis

In addition to repentance, we grow toward theosis by keeping the commandments, especially the greatest one of all: "You should love the Lord your God with all your mind, all your heart, all your soul, all your strength, and your neighbor as yourself."

God is love and can be reached only through love. It is through the practice of love that we achieve the purpose for which we were created: salvation and theosis. And love, the highest of all gifts, is not something that we achieve on own. It is a gift that the Holy Spirit pours into our hearts (Rom. 5:5). Other than love nothing is more divine. It is through the practice of love, above all, that we achieve theosis.

Summarizing what we have said about how to obtain theosis, Bishop Kallistos Ware writes,

> *"The way to deification, to union with God, is to take part in the sacramental life of the church. If a man asks, 'How can I become god?' the answer is very simple: go to church, receive the sacraments regularly, pray to God in spirit and truth, read the Gospels, follow the commandments."*

The True Greatness of Man

Life is not, as Sartre said, a burning theater in which we are trapped with no exit. In His great love for us God has provided an exit. In fact, He Himself is the door that leads homeward. We do not have to run like rats in a maze, up one blind alley after another. The way before us is clear.

As Father A. Calivas has said, "Planted in Christ we become again sons and daughters of God the Father. And in the power of the Holy Spirit, we begin our divine ascent. We begin the ceaseless process by which the image of God is realized in us. We move gradually but certainly from weakness to strength, from sin to holiness, from death to life, from dishonor to honor, and from glory to glory" (II Corinthians 3:18).

The true greatness of man lies in what God has called him to become: god by grace. Man is so great that he can contain God in himself, be united with Him inseparably, and grow into the measure and stature of the Son of

God. We are called to "grow up into Him in all things" (Ephesians 4:15). Our destiny is the highest possible: "We shall be like Him." To see Christ face to face, to be with Him in unbroken fellowship, to be like Him—this is the destiny of every Christian soul. Of all religions, none offers man more respect and dignity than Christianity. And of all Christian traditions none provides man with such a glorious goal as Orthodoxy: theosis, becoming partakers of divine nature. The seeds of greatness were planted within us at Baptism. They need to be nurtured on a daily basis through prayer and the sacraments to help us become what we are, i.e., children of God, heirs of God's kingdom.

There was an argument once among architects as to how high ceilings should be. Some felt that they should not be more than twelve feet high so as not to make the people in them feel inferior or insignificant. Others felt that high ceilings with lofty arches and high domes like St. Sophia in Constantinople and St. Peter's in Rome help people realize that life has a grandeur and a beauty that awakens them to aspire to the highest and the best.

Such is the doctrine of theosis. It does not limit our aspiration to a twelve-foot ceiling, twice the measure of man. Rather, it raises our vision to see our fullest and greatest potential in the command we have received from God to partake of His glory. Thus, theosis will always be the ideal of Orthodoxy and the chief purpose of the Church's existence. It shows us that the soul is capable of far more than we can imagine.

Let me ask you one question: When was the last time your fantastic potential in Christ gave you goose pimples? If it hasn't, it should.

Let me share with you now how many people lose their potential.

Mary-Alice had potential.
It was the first thing anyone noticed when they met her.
"Mary-Alice," they would say, "You've got great potential!"
After a while, Mary-Alice became fright-

ened. *"What if I should lose my potential,"*
she thought.
So Mary-Alice kept her potential stuffed
under her mattress.
She soon discovered that the lump under
the mattress made it difficult to sleep.

Mary-Alice packed up her potential and
took it to a bank on the far side of town.
She rented a large safe-deposit box and
locked her potential away in the vault.
Faithfully, on the third Tuesday of every
month, Mary-Alice would visit her poten-
tial.

Cautiously, she would peek into the box.
Then she would lock it up again and store
her potential safely back in the vault.
Feeling quite content Mary-Alice would
take the bus home,
secure in the knowledge that if nothing
else, she would always have her potential.
      — *Pat Ryan*

Unfortunately, this is what many of us do with our potential; we bury it and lose it! It is obvious that we must either use it or lose it.

The Rich Potential of Theosis

When we were baptized, God placed in us the rich potential of theosis, of sharing in the very life of God through faith, prayer and the sacraments. Again, let me say that theosis—that seemingly difficult word of Orthodox theology—is really a very simple word. It means becoming, becoming more and more like God in Christ as we go through life; becoming all that God wants us to become by His grace, growing to the fullest potential that God intends for us; becoming partakers of God's nature, gods by grace as Jesus is God by nature.

Our true greatness lies in what God has called us to become: gods by grace: "Beloved, we are God's children now; it does not yet appear what we shall be, but we know that when He appears we shall be like Him, for we shall see Him as He is" (I John 3:2).

Prayer

Lord, what am I becoming? I know I'm

becoming older, but am I becoming wiser, more loving, more forgiving, more gracious, more understanding, in a word, more like You. More God-like?

Am I striving to become by grace what you created me to be, or am I denying and covering over Your restored image in me through selfishness and greed?

Help me to aspire to the highest and the best and to use the power you offer me to become truly Your child as I partake more and more of Your love. Amen.

Achieving Your Potential in Christ: Theosis (Part 7)

Not long ago, a young man who had been killed in a motorcycle accident was buried. The Harley-Davidson bike he was riding when he was killed was buried with him. His sobbing mother explained, "It was his whole life!"

How tragic to have a whole life wrapped up in a motorcycle. Yet, if this practice were followed widely, what a strange assortment of burial pieces would be in our cemeteries. One would be buried with his stocks and bonds. Another grave would be crowded with the latest novels and pornographic magazines. Another would be filled with fishing poles, golf clubs and hunting rifles. Still another would have season tickets to all the baseball, football and basketball games.

This leads us to ask: what is life all about? Why are we here? Life is so short. What is it to be used for? Is life to be wasted on motor-cycles or is it to be invested in something? If so, what?

What is Life?

Listen to these definitions of what life is for various people:

Life is "a tale told by an idiot, full of sound and fury, signifying nothing" (Shakes-peare).

"Life is no brief candle to me. It is a sort of splendid torch which I have got hold of for the moment, and I want to make it burn as brightly as possible before handing it on to future generations" (G.B. Shaw).

"Life is like a game of cards: we cannot help the hand that is dealt us, but we can help the way we play it."

"Life is like a voyage in which we choose neither vessel nor weather, but much can be done in the management of the sails and the guidance of the helm."

"You don't get to choose how you're

going to die. Or when. You can only decide how you're going to live. Now." (J. Baez).

Life is a gift to be used every day,
not to be smothered and hidden away;
It isn't a thing to be stored in the chest
Where you gather your keepsakes
and treasure your best;
It isn't a joy to be sipped now and then
And promptly put back in a dark place
again.
Life is a gift that the humblest may boast of
And one that the humblest may well make
the most of.
Get out and live it each hour of the day,
Wear it and use it as much as you may;
Don't keep it in niches and corners and
grooves.
You'll find that in service its beauty im-
proves.   *— Edgar A. Guest*

"Life is a vapor that appears for a little while and then vanishes away" (James 4:14).

"Life is coming from the Father and going to the Father" (Jesus).

"Life is turning everything over to Jesus, taking Him at His word, and entering the open arms of His Love."

"For me to live is Christ, to die is gain" (St. Paul).

We see from these many definitions that life is many things to different people—all the way from "a tale told by an idiot" to "a journey from the Father to the Father."

"For Me to Live is Christ"

Pointing to all that the world had to offer, St. Paul called it "garbage." Health, success, money, pleasure and all the rest — all have to be checked like excess baggage at the door of death. All is decay, rot and stinking decomposition said Paul—garbage! And he went on to say, "For me to live is Christ."

Go through history, pick out some of the great spiritual giants and ask them, "When did you really begin to live?" And one by one they will give the same answer, "When I met Jesus Christ." Whether it be Zacchaeus or Paul or Augustine or Anthony or any of the saints, the answer is the same: "I began to

live—really live—when I met Christ person-
ally, when I became aware of His love for me
and submitted my life to Him."

Helen Keller once said, "I will not just
live my life— I will not just spend my life—I
will invest my life." Life is too precious to be
invested in anyone or anything except in the
Lord Jesus, the Son of the Living God. For,
you see, God loves life. He is the One who
invented life. And it is to the full flowering
of life in theosis that He calls us in and
through His Son, Jesus.

What is Your Plan for Life?

A lot of sales people use this expression,
"If you fail to plan, you plan to fail." If you
don't have a plan for life, you will fail. What
is your plan for life? Do you have one?

"If a man has not discovered something to
life for, he isn't fit to live," someone said.

Two Big Questions

In man's quest for meaning, the two big questions are "Who am I?" and "Why am I here?" For us Orthodox Christians, the first question has been answered by the Holy Trinity. Who am I? "I am one who is loved by God the Father who created me out of nothing. I am one who is loved and redeemed by God the Son, my Precious Jesus, who loved me and gave Himself for me. I am one who is loved and indwelt by God the Holy Spirit, God's power and presence within me." Because of this, I cannot but break out in joy and say, "Blessed Trinity glory to Thee!" The second question, "Why am I here?" is answered by the Great Commandment, "You shall love the Lord your God with all your mind, all your heart, all your soul, all your strength and your neighbor as yourself."

Thus, I am one loved by God, Father, Son and Holy Spirit. And I am placed in this world to love God with all my being and my neighbor as myself.

Why am I here? If God is love, and I am loved by God and placed here to love, then I am here for theosis.

God by Grace

Jesus is the Son of God Who came to reveal to us the height and depth and length and breadth of God's love for us. He is the One Who makes everything fit. He is the One in Whom all things adhere, hold together. To our most profound questions about the meaning of life, He offers the most eloquent answer: Himself: "I am the Way, the Truth and the Life." He assures us that our fondest hopes, our wildest dreams are destined to be fulfilled in Himself. Not content with urging me to be my best self, He gives me visions of being the kind of person I would never have dared to aspire to be: namely, god by grace as He is God by nature.

Why Am I Here?

Why am I here? I am here to know Jesus, whom to know is life eternal. Why am I here? I am here to love Jesus, Whom to love is heaven. Why am I here? I am here to serve Jesus whom to serve is life's greatest joy. Why am I here? I am here for theosis, for sharing in God's eternal glory. The Apostle John writes, "In Him (Christ) was life; and the life was the light of men."

How Much Do You Want to Live?

One day a doctor said to a patient, "How much do you really want to live?" The patient replied, "I want to live more than anything else in the world. I love life." The doctor replied, "Well, then you must stop smoking immediately."

May I ask you the same question, "How much do you really want to live?" If your answer is the same as that of the patient just mentioned, then I would say to you, "You must stop trying to live life alone. You must stop trying to live life selfishly. You must stop living for the trinkets of this life which will one day end up in a garbage dump. You must let the Lord Jesus have first place in your life just as St. Paul did when he said, "It is no longer I who live, but Christ who lives in me; and the life I now live in the flesh I live by faith in the Son of God, who loved me and gave himself for me."

So don't just live your life. Don't just spend your life. Invest your life in Him who alone can give you fullness of joy, life everlasting, and make you a partaker of His divine nature.

Listen to this simple yet profoundly beautiful thought: "Your life is God's gift to you; what you do with your life is your gift to God."

Without God, life has no meaning whatsoever. With God, life has abundant meaning both for now and for all eternity. "He who has the Son has life; he who has not the Son of God has not life" (I John 5:12).

George Maztzarides sums up what we have said about theosis this way,

"According to Palamas, the deification of human nature was accomplished for the first time in the person of Christ... Christ's human nature became the vessel for uncreated divine energy, and henceforth communicates this grace in the Holy Spirit to all believers. Man is reborn through the sacrament of baptism, becomes one flesh with Christ through communion in His deified body, and so participates in His new life and becomes a citizen of the heavenly kingdom. By reason of his unbreakable bond with the source of all true life, he no longer fears death nor directs his life under the shadow of its threat... His main concern during earthly life is to preserve perpetual communion with God through prayer and sacramental life." *

* "The Deification of Christ." G. Mantzarides. SVS Press. Crestwood, NY. 1984. P. 80.

Life is Worth Living

Life is worth living for many reasons. Life is worth living because Christ loves you. Life is worth living because Christ died for you and rose again to give you life. Life is worth living because with Christ, life is both eternal and abundant. But life is worth living, above all, because in Christ your destiny is theosis, becoming Christ-like, god by grace. Therefore choose Christ and live. With Christ, life can be lived meaningfully, divinely, victoriously, and eternally.

Prayer

Heavenly Father, help us to live while we're alive, to live in You and for You, for apart from You there is no life—only death. Truly he who has your Son has life, he who does not have the Son has no life. Help us to accept Your Son and through Him the gift of Your divine life and likeness in theosis. Amen.

The Bible and Theosis

The Bible has much to say about theosis. The most quoted verse for theosis is one which seems rather isolated to some, i.e., II Peter 1:4, "... become partakers of divine nature," or as the NEB translation says "to share in the very being of God." Although II Peter is a very explicit statement about theosis, there are many other verses in the Bible that refer to salvation as "participation" or "sharing" or "fellowship" with God, or "indwelling" in the words of the Gospel of John.

St. Paul says that we are made to be "filled with all the fullness of God" (Ephesians 3:19): what is "being filled with all the fullness of God" but theosis?

The Apostle John writes that God's Son and Spirit have appeared on earth to bring God's people and the world into the fullness of God's being and the life of the Kingdom:

"And the word became flesh and dwelt among us, full of grace and truth, and we beheld His glory, glory as of the only-begotten Son from the Father. . . and of His fullness have we all received, grace upon grace..." (John 1:14-16).

In John 17:22-23 Jesus prays the prayer of theosis: "The glory that Thou hast given me I have given to them that they may be one as we are one: I in them and Thou in Me, that they may be perfectly one." Is not theosis the perfect fulfillment of this prayer of Jesus!

"For you know the grace of our Lord Jesus Christ, that though He was rich, yet for your sake He became poor, so that by His poverty you might become rich" (II Corinthians 2:16).

"There is therefore now no condemnation to those who are in Christ Jesus... But you are not in the flesh, you are in the Spirit, if the Spirit of God really dwells in you. Anyone who does not have the Spirit of Christ does not belong to Him. But if Christ is in you, although your bodies are dead because of your sin, your spirits are alive because of righteousness. If the Spirit of Him Who raised Jesus from the dead dwells in you, He who raised Christ Jesus from the dead will give life to your mortal bodies also through His Spirit which dwells in you" (Romans 8:1, 9:11).

Theosis, participation in the life of God, is further evidenced in verses such as the following which speak of God in us: "We will come and make our home with him" (John 14:23). "It is no longer I who live, but Christ who lives in me" (Galatians 2:20). Paul's desire is that "Christ be formed in you" (Galatians 4:19).

When the Apostle John says that "it does not yet appear what we shall be" He is referring to the future theosis of those who were now made children of God (I John 3:2).

Psalm 82:6 which is quoted by Jesus in John 10:34 is another strong reference to theosis: "I say, you are gods." We see in this verse that even in the Old Testament which is the guardian of monotheism, the word "gods," which Jesus quotes, was applied to people. It speaks of the God-given potential of theosis.

When we unite ourselves unto Christ we become "changed in His likeness from one degree of glory to another; for this comes from the Lord Who is the Spirit" (II Corinthians 3:18).

"Just as we have borne the image of the man of dust, we shall also bear the image of the man of heaven" (I Corinthians 15:4-9).

Christ took His human nature into heaven. There our glorified and deified human nature already stands before the throne of God.

"We have died and our life is hidden with Christ in God" (Colossians 3:3).

"But God, Who is rich in mercy, out of His great love with which He loved us, even when we were dead through our trespasses, made us alive together with Christ and raised us up with him, and made us sit with him in the heavenly places in Christ Jesus" (Ephesians 2:4-6).

"... Christ in you, the hope of glory" (Galatians 1:27). When Christ dwells in us, His presence in us creates a unique "hope of glory." Describing this "hope of glory" C.S. Lewis wrote in his book "The Weight of Glory": "The promise of Scripture may very roughly be reduced to five heads... firstly, that we shall be with Christ; secondly, that we shall be like Him; thirdly... that we shall have 'glory'; fourthly, that we shall in some sense be fed or feasted or entertained; and finally, that we shall have some sort of official position in the universe—ruling cities, judging angels, being pillars of God's temple."

Truly, when we consider God's promise regarding theosis, "it does not yet appear what we shall be."

The author of Hebrews takes this a step further when he speaks of our share in or partaking of "a heavenly calling" (3:1), and he declares that we are made partakers of Christ (3:14) and of the Holy Spirit (6:4). Finally, the apostle Paul again affirms that those who rise in Christ will "put on" God's own incorruptible immortality (1 Cor. 15:52-57; cf. 2 Cor. 4:16-5:8).

St. Paul speaks of the fullness of God's presence abiding in us, when he prays, "The grace of our Lord Jesus Christ and the love of God and the fellowship of the Holy Spirit be with you all" (2 Cor. 13:13).

All these verses constitute only a small part of the many references to theosis found in the scriptures.

Theosis and the Church Fathers

The Church Fathers have much to say about theosis. St. Ignatius of Antioch writes to his correspondents that they are "God bearers" (theophoroi) and "full of God" (Theou gemete). Clement of Alexandria writes, "The Word of God became man in order that you may learn from man how man may become God."

St. Basil writes, "Man is a creature who has received the command to become god." St. Maximus interprets this to mean that we are to "reunite through love the created nature (human) with the uncreated nature (divine grace)."

St. Symeon the New Theologian writes, "We become gods by disposition and grace, heirs of God and joint heirs with Christ, and together with this we receive the mind of Christ; and through it all we see God and

Christ Himself, living in us according to His divinity, moving in a conscious way within us."

"He was made a sharer in our mortality," said Augustine, "He made us sharers in His deity."

St. Gregory, Patriarch of Constantinople writes in one of his "theological orations": "On that day when God will be all in all, we will no longer be captive to our sinful passions, but will be entirely like God, ready to receive into our hearts the whole God and God alone. This is the perfection to which we press on."

The Doxastikon troparion (hymn) of the Praises of the Feast of the Annunciation says,

"Adam of old was deceived:
wanting to be God he failed to be God.
God became man,
so that He may make Adam god."

St. Gregory of Nyssa writes, "Man's life is a strenuous and endless ascent toward God, that is, deification (theosis)."

St. Gregory of Nazianzen writes in his

Easter Oration:

"Yesterday I was crucified with Him; today I am glorified with Him; yesterday I died with Him, today I am quickened with him; yesterday I was buried with Him; today I rise with Him... We have become like Christ, for Christ became like us. We have become gods through Him, for He became man for us."

St. Symeon the New Theologian writes,

"God the Word borrowed flesh from us, which he did not have by nature. He became man, which He was not. To those who believe in Him, He gives His own divinity to share, which neither angel nor man had ever acquired. And men became gods, which they were not, through adoption and grace."

"Man by the grace of God can become that which God is in essence," writes Maximus the Confessor.

St. Gregory of Nyssa says, "We hide within us something which causes us to resemble God, to participate in God; it is indispensable to possess in our being something which conforms us to participation in him."

St. Maximus the Confessor again: "God has created us in order that we may become partakers of the Divine Nature, that we may enter into eternity, that we may resemble Him, that is, being deified by His grace through which all things were made."

St. Athanasios summarizes it all:

"The Son of God became the Son of Man in order that the sons of men, the sons of Adam, might be made the sons of God. The Logos who was begotten of the Father in heaven in an ineffable... eternal manner, came to this earth to be born of the Virgin Mary, the Theotokos, in order that they who were born of earth might be born again of God... He took upon himself our baseness and our poverty that He might bestow on us his wealth. His passion is his impassibility. His death is our immortality. His tears our joy, His burial our resurrection and His baptism our sanctification. His bruises are our salvation. His chastisement our peace. His ignominy is our glory. His abasement is our ascension."

A major theme in the Cappadocian Fathers is the idea of the human person as a free-willed receptacle called to fill itself by participating in divine life through prayer and the sacraments and to pour forth that life again in love.

Man Does Not Become a God

We live in a day when popular psychology and the cults are propagating the deity of man by teaching people to say, "I am everywhere. I am omniscient. I am God." People pay expensively to enroll in seminars which tell them, "You are a supreme being. There is no death; man is God; knowledge of self is salvation and power." A famous actress and her spiritual advisor, for example, stand on Malibu Beach and, with their arms flung open to the cosmos, shout, "I am God! I am God! I am God!"

Obviously, this is not what we mean by theosis. In Orthodox theology, this is heresy of the very first order. Lucifer tried to become God and was thrown out of heaven because of it (Isaiah 14:12-15).

Commenting on the meaning of the expression "partakers of divine nature," William Barclay says:

"Sometimes in Greek, when a noun is used without the definite article, it has a kind of adjectival force. To say that man could become <u>ho theos</u> would be to say that man can become identical with God, one and the same as God. But to say that a man can become <u>theos</u>—using the word without the definite article—is to say that a man can come to have the same kind of life and existence and being as God has, but without becoming identical with God. The conception of deification is that man through Jesus Christ can be lifted out of the life of the fallen and corrupt humanity into the very life of God." [*]

Thus, in theosis man does not "possess" God nor does he become God in essence. Rather, he participates in that which is given to him, thanking God for His ineffable grace.

Theosis in no way means that human be-

[*]   "The Mind of Christ," Wm. Barclay. Harper and Brothers. NY. 1960. P. 260

ings "become God" in a pantheistic sense. It means, rather, that believers enter into a personal relationship with God through Baptism and participate fully in God's life through prayer and the sacraments.

What Theosis is Not

When foster parents adopt children they are not able to grant to the adopted child their nature, their blood and genes. But in divine adoption which is a prolongation of the Incarnation, we become partakers of divine nature. Yet how can man partake of God's nature?

The Church Fathers distinguish between the nature or essence of God and His energies. The nature of God is both participable and unparticipable. It is participable in the uncreated energies but not in its essence. Thus, theosis is not participation in the divine essence. For if we could unite with God's essence, as Vladimir Lossky states, we would cease to be creatures and God would be not a Trinity of Persons but would have as many hypostases as there are persons participating in His essence. Thus, unity with God in theosis is not pantheism, which believes that everything is God.

St. Gregory Palamas delineates as follows between the essence of God and His energies: "God in His completeness deifies those who are worthy of this, by uniting Himself with them, not hypostatically—that belonged to Christ alone—not essentially, but through a small part of the uncreated energies... while yet being entirely present in each."

Commenting on II Peter 1:4, St. Nicodemus the Hagiorite wrote:

"But whoever hears the Chief Apostle (Peter) saying that it has been granted to Christians to be communicants of Divine Nature, let him not be deceived and think he is saying that anyone can partake of the Nature and Essence of God— perish the thought! For this is impossible for a rational creature... Because... the infinite Essence and Nature of God is not only unparticipable by creatures, but is also invisible to them, and not only invisible, but also incomprehensible, and in all respects inscrutable and unfathomable. Therefore the

communion of the divine of which the Chief Apostle here speaks is, namely, that those Christians who have been purified... will communicate and partake of God's... energies and powers and graces."

What do we mean when we speak of God's "energies?"

Here are some answers.

Divine energies are God Himself as He has manifested Himself to us. They are the ways by which God has come down to us and revealed Himself. Through His energies God continues to enter into relationship with people. By grace, that is by God's energies, we are no longer separated from God. His energies are the power of His grace which is experienced by believers today and is called theosis. The vision of the uncreated light experienced by the Hesychasts is a form of God's energies, just as was the light which shown through Christ at the Transfiguration. Grace is understood by the Orthodox as the energies of God in action, making God known and present to us. And grace continuously granted and accepted, results in theosis.

The Christian virtues are ultimately divine energies in which human beings are called to participate. Patience, for example, is a divine energy in which we are called to share through the Holy Spirit. So are love, joy, peace, gentleness, kindness and self-control. These virtues do not emanate from us but are fruits or energies of the Holy Spirit in us. They are the evidence of the reality of our participation in theosis now. The Church Fathers stress that to exercise any one virtue perfectly, be it forgiveness, or patience or self-control, requires all the virtues.

God is by nature unknowable in His essence. He becomes knowable through His energies, which are the ways by which He, in His grace, has opened Himself to us. "No one has ever seen God; the only Son, Who is in the bosom of the Father, He has made Him known" (John 1:18). Although not capable of knowing God in His essence, we are capable of knowing Him through His energies, since He is present in each of His energies.

When we speak of theosis, then, we mean a union with the energies of God and not with the essence of God, which always remains hidden and unknown. Yet this is a true union with God in which God and man retain their unique characteristics.

St. Basil has written, "We know our God from His energies, but we do not claim that we can draw near to His essence, for His energies come down to us, but His essence remains unapproachable" (Letter 234, 1. PG 32, 869).

Man's knowledge of God can be only of His energies, not of His essence. All of us participate in God's energies but each one of us differently. Deified humanity is united to God only in grace and energy. George Mantzaridis writes, "Man's deification is not realized through participation in God's essence but through communion in His divine energy. Man may share in God's glory and brightness, but the divine essence remains inaccessible and nonparticipable. Thus the deified man is made god in all things, but he neither is identified with the divine essence nor shares it."[*]

John Breck summarizes the distinction between the essence and the energies of God as follows:

"... taking up the distinction between essence and energies that goes back at least to Saint Gregory of Nyssa, the Greek patristic tradition affirms that deification is achieved by grace, through the sanctifying power of the divine energies. Humans are not, nor can we ever be 'participants of the divine nature', if by nature we understand not 'being' (as 2 Pet. 1:4) but the divine essence. For the latter is transcendent and inaccessible to any form of created reality. 'Deification,' therefore, does not suggest that we become God, despite the rather audacious language used by some

[*] "The Deification of Man," G. Mantzaridis. SVS Press, Crestwood, NY. 1984. P. 122.

of the early patristic writers. It means that by the initiative that belongs wholly to the three Divine Persons, humans as creatures are introduced into personal relationships of participation in the un-created, divine energies or grace. Thereby people become 'by grace' what God is 'by nature.'*

---

*   "Salvation in Christ: An Orthodox-Lutheran Dialogue",
    Meyendorff and Tobias. Augsburg Publ. House. Mpls, MN. 1992.

Bishop Ware's
Five Points on Theosis

Bishop Ware helps us better understand theosis by making the following five points:

Firstly, theosis is not reserved for a select few special saints. It is something in which all baptized and chrismated Christians are called to share. If we love God, keep His commandments, rise as often as we fall (through repentance), we are already in the process of being deified.

Secondly, being deified does not mean that we cease to be conscious of sin. Theosis not only presupposes a continual act of repentance, but also sensitizes us to sin so that we are in a constant state of penitence. That is why we continue to pray the Jesus Prayer to the very end of our lives: "Lord Jesus, Son of God, have mercy on me, the sinner."

Thirdly, there is nothing extraordinary about the methods we follow to achieve theosis. We continue to participate in the liturgy every week, receive the sacraments regularly, pray, read God's word and obey God's commandments.

Fourthly, there is nothing solitary about theosis. It presupposes love of God and love of neighbor. "There is nothing selfish about deification," writes Bishop Ware, "for only if he loves his neighbor can a man be deified." "From our neighbor is life and from our neighbor is death," said St. Anthony.

Fifthly, as an expression of love of God and love of man, theosis is very practical. It includes not only silence and prayer but also caring for the sick in the hospital of Caesarea as did St. Basil, and helping the poor of Alexandria as did St. John the Almsgiver, etc. [*]

---

[*] "The Orthodox Church," T. Ware. Penguin Books. Baltimore, MD. 1963. P. 246-247.

Our Goal in Life: Theosis

Zen Buddhism says, "In the beginning there was nothing. The purpose of life is to achieve union with nothingness." Orthodox Christianity says, "In the beginning there was God. The purpose of life is to achieve union with God not in His essence but through His energies."

Solzhenitsyn said once regarding our goal in life, "The meaning of earthly existence lies, not as we have grown used to thinking, in prospering, but in the development of the soul." I would add, "In the development of the soul toward theosis, toward becoming like God in Christ, toward sharing in His glory." This and none other is our great goal in life as we see in the story of creation when God said, "Let us make man in our image and likeness" (Genesis 1:26). A thing is perfect (teleion) if it realizes the purpose (telos) for which it was made. Man is perfect if he realizes the goal for which he was made: to become like God.

One day an older person asked a student, "What are you going to be when you grow up?" The student promptly replied, "A veterinarian." The older person replied, "I didn't ask you what you were going to do, but what you are going to be."

Often in life we confuse what we do with what we are. But the really important thing in life is not what we do for a living but what we are called to be: partakers of divine nature, becoming like God. "Be ye holy as I am holy," said the Lord. For Orthodox Christianity theosis is the final goal and the highest vocation of man and woman.

Thomas Merton wrote in his book "No Man Is An Island":

"Each one of us has some kind of vocation. We are all called by God to share in His life and in His kingdom. Each one of us is called to a special place in the Kingdom. If we find that place we will be happy. If we do not find it we can never be completely happy.

For each one of us, there is only one thing necessary; to fulfill our own destiny, according to God's will, to be what God wants us to be."

God wants us to be like Him, to share in His love, glory and peace.

Christ holds up before us not only a mirror to help us see ourselves as we truly are (sinners); He also holds up before us an icon (Himself) to show us what we can become by God's grace, sons and daughters of God, partakers of divine nature.

The aim of the Christian life, which St. Seraphim of Sarov described as the acquisition of the Holy Spirit, can be defined equally well in terms of theosis, becoming like God, sharing His divine nature, since the purpose of the Holy Spirit in us is to deify us, to make us Temples of God's presence.

St. Athanasius said, "God became man so that man might become god (or divine)." This expresses the basic Orthodox conviction that our purpose in life, the ultimate reason for our being, is to become by grace what

God is by nature.

In the words of Vladimir Lossky:

*Thus the redeeming work of Christ...
is to be directly related to the ultimate
goal of creatures: to know union with
God. If this union has been accomplished in the divine person of the Son,
who is God become man, it is necessary
that each human person, in turn, should
become god by grace, or "a partaker of
the divine nature," according to Saint
Peter's expression.*